CUPCAKES &
COCKTAILS

About Bonnie Marcus

Bonnie Marcus launched her stylish stationery company, the Bonnie Marcus Collection "where fashion meets paper®," in 2002 from her dining room table, while expecting her first child. As a former wedding planner in New York City, Marcus was well-known for her event planning expertise and found there was a void in the stationery market in terms of fashion-forward stylish designs. She decided to combine her passion for fashion (having worked for designer Diane Von Furstenberg) with her love of event planning and her collection took the stationery industry by storm! Bonnie's stylish designs are now available in thousands of retail stores worldwide and celebrity fans include Cindy Crawford, Christina Aguilera, Britney Spears, Eva Longoria, Marcia Cross, and many others. Marcus has been recognized as a pioneer for women in business and is proud to be an established partner of the Breast Cancer Research Foundation® and Autism Speaks®. For further information about the company, please visit www.bonniemarcus.com.

Bennie Marcus Collection

CUPCAKES &
COCKTAILS

FABULOUS CUPCAKE AND COCKTAIL RECIPES FOR ANY OCCASION

Bath • New York • Singapore • Hong Kong • Cologne • Delhi
Melbourne • Amsterdam • Johannesburg • Shenzhen

This edition published by Parragon Books Ltd in 2013 and distributed by

Parragon Inc.
440 Park Avenue South, 13th Floor
New York, NY 10016
www.parragon.com

Project managed by Annabel King
Additional text by Robin Donovan
Internal design by Lisa McCormick

ISBN 978-1-4723-2977-6

Printed in China

Notes for the Reader

This book uses standard kitchen measuring spoons and cups. All spoon and cup measurements are level unless otherwise indicated. Unless otherwise stated, milk is assumed to be whole, eggs are large, individual vegetables are medium, and pepper is freshly ground black pepper. Unless otherwise stated, all root vegetables should be peeled prior to using.

Garnishes, decorations, and serving suggestions are all optional and not necessarily included in the recipe ingredients or method. The times given are only an approximate guide. Preparation times differ according to the techniques used by different people and the cooking times may also vary from those given. Optional ingredients, variations, or serving suggestions have not been included in the time calculations.

Contents

Cupcakes and Cocktails
Introduction

Like whiskers on kittens and brown paper packages tied up with string, cupcakes and cocktails are two of our favorite things. Happily, we're not alone in our love of fanciful alcoholic beverages and whimsical single-serving cakes. Both have enjoyed a surge in popularity in recent years, spawning entirely new cultures of studied aficionados and devoted fans. And, let's face it, few things have more appeal. Properly made and adorned, both are a feast for the eyes and the palate.

Combining these two popular cultural phenomena can make for a uniquely modern take on the old standbys of drinks and hors d'oeuvres, wine and cheese, or pretzels and beer. Think up any excuse for a party and break out the baking pans and shakers to combine these two hot trends in one colorful, delicious spread. Even if you can't drum up a good reason to celebrate, cocktails and cupcakes, all on their own, are welcome excuses for a luxuriously cozy night in. Here, you'll find recipes for both cupcakes and cocktails, as well as theme and decorating ideas to strike just the right note for any occasion.

Cupcakes are one of the world's most perfect foods—sinfully decadent, delightfully delicious, and made in perfectly portioned individual servings. And, as a lucky bonus, each and every one delivers the perfect ratio of frosting to cake. With the endless possibilities for flavor combinations and themes, they are as much fun to bake and decorate as they are to eat. Here, you'll find cupcakes in a range of flavors, some based on cocktail recipes (and with the booze baked right in) and some designed simply to be the perfect match for a well-mixed drink. And, as an added bonus, we've also added in some delicious dessert recipes!

Once baked, cupcakes are a blank canvas ready to be adorned in honor of whatever you want to celebrate—an engagement, wedding, anniversary, new job, new house, or even just to reward yourself for getting through another long day at work.

Cocktails, too, allow for a ton of creativity, from flavor combining to garnishing. Whether you're going for a "fun with the girls" vibe or something more romantic, there's a cupcake-and-cocktail combination that will set just the right tone.

Whatever the occasion—whether you're entertaining a crowd or simply craving a sweet treat on a quiet night in—get creative, mixing and matching flavors and decorations.

The Perfect Combination

Pairing decadent cupcakes and fancy cocktails is an amazing way to set the mood, whether a quiet night in, a casual gathering of close friends, or even a blowout bash.

For a casual night in, there is nothing better than a cupcake and cocktail. They offer an easy, single serving of luxury that cannot be beaten. Perfectly baked cupcakes, swirls of frosting, encased in a pretty paper wrapper, all make for cupcakes that look as good as they taste. Serve with a cocktail that complements the delicate flavors of the cupcake and you've got a perfect treat.

If you're throwing a party, a cupcake-and-cocktail-inspired theme will allow you to break out the glam without breaking the bank. Keep it simple by choosing one or two signature drinks instead of trying to mix a full bar to order. Start by choosing a theme—anything from tropical luau to retro chic—and then plan your food, beverages, decor, and music or other entertainment to match.

Martini

INGREDIENTS
serves 1
2½ ounces gin
1 teaspoon dry vermouth,
    or to taste
cocktail olive, to decorate

METHOD
1 Put cracked ice into a
cocktail shaker.

2 Pour the gin and vermouth
over the ice.

3 Shake until well frosted.
Strain into a chilled
cocktail glass.

4 Decorate with the olive.

Apple Martini

INGREDIENTS
serves 1
¾ ounce vodka
¾ ounce sour apple schnapps
¾ ounce apple juice

METHOD

1 Put cracked ice into a cocktail shaker and pour in the vodka, schnapps, and apple juice.

2 Shake vigorously until well frosted.

3 Strain into a chilled cocktail glass.

Caramel Appletini Cupcakes

INGREDIENTS
makes 12

1½ cups all-purpose flour
1½ teaspoons baking powder
1 teaspoon ground ginger
1 teaspoon ground cinnamon
⅛ teaspoon ground nutmeg
¼ teaspoon salt
1 stick unsalted butter, softened
1 cup superfine sugar or
    granulated sugar
1 teaspoon vanilla extract
2 extra-large eggs
¼ cup applesauce
2 tablespoons apple juice
2 tablespoons apple vodka

frosting

1 stick unsalted butter, softened
1 cup firmly packed dark
    brown sugar
⅓ cup heavy cream
pinch of salt
2 tablespoons apple-flavored
    vodka
1½–2 cups confectioners' sugar
    (see method)

to decorate

green food coloring
2 ounces marzipan
1 ounce brown ready-to-use
    fondant

METHOD

1 Preheat the oven to 350°F and line a 12-cup cupcake pan with paper liners.

2 Sift together the flour, baking powder, ginger, cinnamon, nutmeg, and salt in a bowl. Put the butter and sugar into a separate bowl and beat until pale and fluffy. Add the vanilla extract, then add the eggs, one at a time, beating after each addition. Add half of the flour mixture and the applesauce, apple juice, and vodka and beat well. Add the remaining flour mixture and mix.

3 Spoon the batter into the paper liners and bake in the preheated oven for 20 minutes, until a toothpick inserted into the center of a cupcake comes out clean. Let cool in the pan for 1–2 minutes, then transfer to a wire rack to cool completely.

4 To make the frosting, first make a caramel sauce by melting the butter in a small saucepan over medium heat. Add the brown sugar, cream, and salt and cook, stirring constantly, for about 4 minutes, until the sugar has completely dissolved. Remove from the heat, stir in the vodka, and set aside to cool for 30 minutes.

5 Pour the caramel sauce into a mixing bowl, reserving ½ cup to decorate the cupcakes. Add 1½ cups of the confectioners' sugar to the mixing bowl and beat until fully incorporated. Add more confectioners' sugar as needed to achieve a piping consistency. Spoon the frosting into a pastry bag fitted with a star-shape tip and pipe onto the cupcakes.

6 To make the marzipan apple decorations, add a couple of drops of food coloring to the marzipan and knead until the color is evenly incorporated. Roll the marzipan into 12 balls. Pinch off a small amount of fondant and shape into an apple stem. Press into the top of a marzipan ball and repeat for the 11 remaining balls. To serve, drizzle the cupcakes with the reserved caramel sauce and place a marzipan apple on top of each.

Perfect with
a margarita
cupcake!

Margarita

INGREDIENTS
serves 1
2 lime wedges
kosher salt
2½ ounces white tequila
¾ ounce triple sec or Cointreau
1¾ ounces lime juice

METHOD

1 Rub the rim of a chilled cocktail glass with a lime wedge, then dip in a saucer of kosher salt to frost.

2 Put cracked ice into a cocktail shaker. Pour the tequila, triple sec, and lime juice over the ice. Shake vigorously until frosted.

3 Strain into the glass and dress with a lime wedge.

Margarita Cupcakes

INGREDIENTS
makes 12

1½ cups all-purpose flour
1½ teaspoons baking powder
¼ teaspoon salt
1 stick unsalted butter, softened
1 cup superfine sugar or
    granulated sugar

2 teaspoons vanilla extract
2 extra-large eggs
⅓ cup milk
3 tablespoons tequila
finely grated juice and
    zest of 1 lime

frosting
3 extra-large egg whites
¾ cup granulated sugar
2 sticks unsalted butter, softened
¼ cup triple sec
zest of 1 lime
green food coloring

METHOD

1 Preheat the oven to 350°F and line a 12-cup cupcake pan with paper liners.

2 Sift together the flour, baking powder, and salt into a bowl. Put the butter and sugar into a separate bowl and beat until pale and fluffy. Add the vanilla extract and the eggs, one at a time, beating after each addition. Add half of the flour mixture and the milk, tequila, and lime zest and juice and beat until combined. Add the remaining flour mixture and mix.

3 Spoon the batter into the paper liners and bake in the preheated oven for 20 minutes, until a toothpick inserted into the center of a cupcake comes out clean. Let cool in the pan for 1–2 minutes, then transfer to a wire rack to cool completely.

4 To make the frosting, put the egg whites and sugar in the top of a double boiler (or use a heatproof bowl set over a saucepan of gently simmering water) and whisk over simmering water until the sugar has completely dissolved. Remove from the heat and whisk the mixture for 4–5 minutes. Add the butter, 2 tablespoons at a time, and continue to whisk until the mixture holds stiff peaks. Add the triple sec, lime zest, and 2 drops of food coloring and stir until just combined.

5 Spoon the frosting into a pastry bag fitted with a star-shape tip and pipe onto the cupcakes.

Daiquiri

INGREDIENTS
serves 1

1¾ ounces white rum
¾ ounce lime juice
½ teaspoon superfine sugar
   dissolved in 1 tablespoon
   boiling water

METHOD

1 Put cracked ice into a cocktail shaker. Pour the ingredients over the ice. Shake vigorously until well frosted.

2 Strain into a chilled cocktail glass.

Frozen Pineapple Daiquiri

INGREDIENTS
serves 1
1¾ ounces white rum
¾ ounce lime juice
½ teaspoon pineapple syrup
⅓ cup finely chopped pineapple
pineapple wedges, to decorate

METHOD
1 Mix crushed ice in a blender with the other ingredients until slushy. Pour into a chilled cocktail glass. Dress with some pineapple wedges.

Raspberry Daiquiri Cupcakes

INGREDIENTS
makes 12

1½ cups all-purpose flour
1½ teaspoons baking powder
¼ teaspoon salt
1 stick unsalted butter, softened
1 cup superfine sugar or
   granulated sugar
2 extra-large eggs
½ cup milk
2 tablespoons rum
finely grated zest and juice
   of 1 lime

filling

2¾ cups fresh raspberries,
   pureed
¼ cup superfine sugar or
   granulated sugar
2 tablespoons rum
1 tablespoon cornstarch

frosting

1 stick unsalted butter, softened
2–3 cups confectioners' sugar
   (see method)
1 teaspoon raspberry extract
2 tablespoons heavy cream
pinch of salt
pink sugar crystals, to decorate

METHOD

1 Preheat the oven to 350°F and line a 12-cup cupcake pan with paper liners.

2 Sift together the flour, baking powder, and salt in a bowl. Put the butter and sugar into a separate bowl and beat until pale and fluffy. Add the eggs, one at a time, beating after each addition. Add half of the flour mixture, the milk, rum, and lime zest and juice and beat until incorporated. Add the remaining flour mixture and mix.

3 Spoon the batter into the paper liners and bake in the preheated oven for 20 minutes, until a toothpick inserted in the center of a cupcake comes out clean. Let cool in the pan for 1–2 minutes, then transfer to a wire rack to cool completely.

4 To make the filling, put the raspberry puree and sugar into a saucepan and bring to a boil, stirring frequently. Put the rum and cornstarch into a small bowl and whisk together. Pour into the boiling raspberry mixture and cook for another 1–2 minutes, stirring, until the mixture thickens. Remove from the heat and cool, then chill.

5 To make the frosting, use an electric mixer to beat butter until pale and creamy. Add 2 cups of the confectioners' sugar and the remaining ingredients (except the sugar crystals) and 2 tablespoons of the raspberry filling. Beat until well combined. Add more confectioners' sugar, if necessary, to achieve a piping consistency. Spoon the frosting into a pastry bag fitted with a star-shape tip.

6 Use an apple corer to remove the center of each cupcake and spoon the raspberry filling into each hole. Pipe the frosting onto the cupcakes, then sprinkle with the sugar crystals to serve.

When thinking about pairing cupcakes and cocktails, whatever the occasion, there are certain themes that will always be a hit. Summertime begs for the bright flavors of fruit and light, refreshing, citrusy cocktails, while winter nights call for warming flavors, such as cinnamon in a cocktail like Caramel Appletini. Likewise, if you're dreaming of making an escape to a warm, sunny Caribbean island, tropical cocktails and Latin flavors, such as a minty Mojito paired with Coconut & Pineapple Macarons, would be just the thing to transport you there.

Another way to approach pairing is to match flavor profiles. The citrus notes of a Sidecar or Singapore Sling will echo the citrus notes in the Lemon and White Chocolate Creams, while the white chocolate adds a luxuriously rich base. The bracing sour-and-bitter notes of a Cosmopolitan are a great foil for sweet-tangy Limoncello Cupcakes.

And, of course, we can't leave out the classic pairing of chocolate and strawberries. A Strawberrini or Strawberry Colada would both be a perfect match for our Chocolate & Pink Peppercorn Cupcakes. Or pair a Chocolate Martini or Chocolate Diva with our Strawberry Mimosa Cupcakes.

Whatever your perfect combination is, a sweet cupcake and a well-mixed cocktail will set the tone for a fabulous time.

Cosmopolitan Cupcakes

INGREDIENTS
makes 12

1½ cups all-purpose flour
1½ teaspoons baking powder
¼ teaspoon salt
1 stick unsalted butter, softened
1 cup superfine sugar or
    granulated sugar
1 teaspoon vanilla extract
2 extra-large eggs
1 tablespoon lime juice
1 teaspoon finely grated
    lime zest
2 tablespoons cranberry vodka
1 tablespoon Cointreau or
    triple sec
¼ cup milk
pink food coloring

frosting

1 stick unsalted butter, softened
2–2½ cups confectioners' sugar
    (see method)
2 tablespoons cranberry vodka
1 teaspoon vanilla extract
 pink food coloring

to decorate

pink sugar crystals
4 ounces marzipan
green gel food coloring
a green edible-ink marker
12 cocktail umbrellas

METHOD

1 Preheat the oven to 350°F. Line a 12-cup cupcake pan with paper liners.

2 Sift together the flour, baking powder, and salt in a bowl. Put the butter and sugar into a separate bowl and beat until pale and fluffy. Add the vanilla extract, then add the eggs, one at a time, beating after each addition. Add the lime juice, lime zest, vodka, Cointreau or triple sec, milk, and half of the flour mixture and beat until combined. Add the remaining flour mixture and mix well. Stir in a few drops of food coloring and beat until evenly incorporated.

3 Spoon the batter into the paper liners and bake in the preheated oven for 20 minutes, until a toothpick inserted into the center of a cupcake comes out clean. Let cool in the pan for 1–2 minutes, then transfer to a wire rack to cool completely.

4 To make the frosting, put the butter into a bowl and beat with an electric mixer until pale and creamy. Add 2 cups of the confectioners' sugar along with the vodka and vanilla extract. Beat together until well combined. Add more confectioners' sugar as needed to achieve a piping consistency. Add a few drops of food coloring and mix until evenly incorporated.

5 Spoon the frosting into a pastry bag fitted with a star-shape tip. Pipe the frosting onto the cupcakes and sprinkle with the pink sugar crystals to decorate.

6 To make the lime-wedge decorations, divide the marzipan in half. Add a few drops of green food coloring to one half and knead until evenly incorporated. Add more color, if needed, to achieve a dark green color; this will be used to make the lime zest. Add a couple of drops of green food coloring to the remaining piece of marzipan and knead until evenly incorporated; this will be used to make the inside of the lime wedge, so it should be light green.

7 Divide both marzipan colors into 12 pieces. Take one piece of light green marzipan and shape into a semicircle about ¼ inch thick. Lightly pinch the flat side of the semicircle to make a wedge shape. Flatten a piece of the dark green marzipan and press in place around the curved edge of the light green wedge, trimming, as necessary, to give the effect of a zest. Repeat with the remaining marzipan to make 12 lime wedges in total. Using the edible-ink marker, draw lines on the lighter green part to represent the inner membrane of a lime wedge. Set aside to dry.

8 To serve, place a lime wedge on top of each cupcake and insert a cocktail umbrella.

Cosmopolitan

INGREDIENTS
serves 1
1¾ ounces vodka
¾ ounce triple sec
¾ ounce lime juice
¾ ounce cranberry juice
orange peel strip, to decorate

METHOD
1 Put cracked ice into a
cocktail shaker.

2 Pour the liquid ingredients
over the ice.

3 Shake vigorously until
well frosted.

4 Strain into a chilled cocktail
glass and decorate with the
orange peel.

White Cosmopolitan

INGREDIENTS
serves 1

1¼ ounces limoncello
½ ounce Cointreau
½ ounce white cranberry
    and grape juice
dash orange bitters
cranberries, to decorate

METHOD

1 Put cracked ice into a cocktail shaker. Pour the limoncello, Cointreau, and cranberry and grape juice over the ice. Shake vigorously until well frosted.

2 Strain into a chilled glass.

3 Add the bitters and dress with the cranberries.

Limoncello Cupcakes

INGREDIENTS
makes 12

1½ cups all-purpose flour
1½ teaspoons baking powder
¼ teaspoon salt
1 stick unsalted butter, softened
1 cup superfine sugar or
   granulated sugar

2 extra-large eggs
finely grated zest and juice
   of 1 lemon
¼ cup milk
rainbow sprinkles, to decorate

frosting

3 extra-large egg whites
¾ cup superfine sugar or
   granulated sugar
2 sticks unsalted butter, softened
¼ cup limoncello
finely grated zest of 1 lemon

METHOD

1. Preheat the oven to 350°F and line a 12-cup cupcake pan with paper liners.

2. Sift together the flour, baking powder, and salt in a bowl. Put the butter and sugar into a separate bowl and beat until pale and fluffy. Add the eggs, one at a time, beating after each addition. Add half of the flour mixture, the lemon zest and juice, and milk and beat until incorporated. Add the remaining flour mixture and mix.

3. Spoon the batter into the paper liners and bake in the preheated oven for 20 minutes, until a toothpick inserted into the center of a cupcake comes out clean. Remove from the oven and let cool in the pan for 1–2 minutes, then transfer to a wire rack to cool completely.

4. To make the frosting, put the egg whites and sugar in the top of a double boiler (or use a heatproof bowl set over a saucepan of gently simmering water) and whisk over simmering water until the sugar has completely dissolved. Remove from the heat and whisk the mixture for 4–5 minutes. Add the butter, 2 tablespoons at a time, and continue to beat until it holds stiff peaks. Add the limoncello and lemon zest and beat until just combined.

5. Spoon the frosting into a pastry bag fitted with a star-shape tip and pipe the frosting onto the cupcakes. Top with the rainbow sprinkles and serve.

Sidecar

INGREDIENTS
serves 1

1¾ ounces brandy
¾ ounce triple sec
¾ ounce lemon juice
orange peel strip, to decorate

METHOD

1 Put cracked ice into a cocktail shaker, then pour the liquid ingredients over the ice.

2 Shake vigorously until well frosted.

3 Strain into a chilled cocktail glass and decorate with the orange peel.

Singapore Sling

INGREDIENTS
serves 1
1¾ ounces gin
¾ ounce cherry brandy
¾ ounce lemon juice
1 teaspoon grenadine
club soda
lime peel strips and cocktail
    cherries, to decorate

METHOD
1 Put cracked ice into a
cocktail shaker, then pour
the gin over the ice.

2 Add the cherry brandy,
lemon juice, and grenadine
and shake vigorously until
well frosted.

3 Fill a chilled glass halfway
with cracked ice and strain
the cocktail over it.

4 Fill up with club soda and
decorate with the lime peel
and cherries.

Lemon & White Chocolate Creams

INGREDIENTS
makes 12

10 ounces white chocolate, coarsely chopped

2 tablespoons heavy cream

finely grated rind of 1 lemon

2 tablespoons limoncello

4 tablespoons unsalted butter, softened and diced

3 tablespoons finely chopped pistachio nuts

METHOD

1 Put 4 ounces of the chocolate and all the cream in the top of a double boiler (or use a heatproof bowl set over a saucepan of gently simmering water) and heat until melted.

2 Remove from the heat, add the lemon rind, limoncello, and butter, and beat for 3–4 minutes, or until thickened. Transfer to an airtight container and chill in the refrigerator for 6–8 hours, or until firm.

3 Line a baking sheet with nonstick parchment paper. Scoop teaspoonfuls of the mixture and, using the palms of your hands, roll them into truffle-size balls. Place the balls on the prepared baking sheet, cover with plastic wrap, and freeze for 6–8 hours.

4 Put the remaining chocolate in top of a double boiler (or use a heatproof bowl set over a saucepan of gently simmering water) and heat until melted. Using two forks, dip each truffle into the chocolate to coat evenly. Return them to the prepared baking sheet, sprinkle the pistachios over them, and chill in the refrigerator for 1–2 hours, or until firm. Store in an airtight container in the refrigerator for up to five days.

Your cupcakes and frosting can be made ahead of time. Store both the unfrosted cupcakes and the frosting covered in the refrigerator for up to three days. Frost the cupcakes up to 8 hours before party time and store them at room temperature.

If you've whipped up a batch of cupcakes for yourself, rest assured that you don't have to eat them all in one go! Put them into the freezer and you'll have them ready for a treat any time you like. To freeze, wrap unfrosted cupcakes in plastic wrap or in a resealable, freezer-safe plastic bag, and freeze for up to 3 months. To defrost, unwrap the cupcakes and let them thaw at room temperature for about an hour.

Most frostings, too, can be frozen. Freeze them in a resealable, freezer-safe bag and defrost by placing them in the refrigerator for a few hours. Knead the bag to soften the frosting, if necessary, then spread on your cupcakes or transfer to a pastry bag for piping.

Many of your drink ingredients and garnishes can be prepped ahead of time, as well. For instance, you can peel, slice, or dice fruits and make a simple syrup steeped with herbs or other flavors well before you need them, whether for a party or to whip up a quick drink for yourself. Many cocktails can be premixed in large batches, stored in pitchers in the refrigerator, and then poured over ice or whipped up in a blender just before serving.

Long Island Iced Tea

INGREDIENTS
serves 1
1¾ ounces vodka
¾ ounce gin
¾ ounce white tequila
¾ ounce white rum
½ ounce white crème
   de menthe
1¾ ounces lemon juice
1 teaspoon superfine sugar
cola
lime wedge, to decorate

METHOD
1 Put cracked ice into a cocktail shaker. Pour all the liquid ingredients except the cola over the ice, add the sugar, and shake vigorously until well frosted.

2 Fill a tall glass halfway with cracked ice and strain the cocktail over the ice.

3 Fill up with cola.

4 Decorate with the lime wedge.

Manhattan

INGREDIENTS
serves 1
dash Angostura bitters
2½ ounces rye whiskey
¾ ounce sweet vermouth
cocktail cherry, to decorate

METHOD
1 Put cracked ice into a cocktail shaker.

2 Pour the liquid ingredients over the ice.

3 Shake vigorously until well frosted.

4 Strain into a chilled cocktail glass and decorate with the cherry.

Malibu Bay Cupcakes

INGREDIENTS
makes 12

½ cup cranberry juice
1 cup plus 2 tablespoons
    superfine sugar or
    granulated sugar
1½ cups all-purpose flour
1½ teaspoons baking powder
¼ teaspoon salt
1 stick unsalted butter, softened
2 extra-large eggs
½ cup coconut milk
2 tablespoons white rum
2 tablespoons dried cranberries,
    chopped

frosting

3 extra-large egg whites
¾ cup superfine sugar or
    granulated sugar
2 sticks unsalted butter, softened
3 tablespoons white rum
1 tablespoon coconut extract

to decorate

½ cup unsweetened shredded
    dried coconut
pink food coloring
12 cocktail straws

METHOD

1 Preheat the oven to 350°F and line a 12-cup cupcake pan with paper liners.

2 Combine the cranberry juice and 2 tablespons of the sugar in a small saucepan and bring to a boil over medium–high heat. Boil for about 10 minutes, until reduced to about 2 tablespoons. Set aside to cool.

3 Sift together the flour, baking powder, and salt in a bowl. Put the butter and remaining sugar into a separate bowl and beat until pale and fluffy. Add the eggs, one at a time, beating after each addition. Add half the flour mixture, the cranberry reduction, coconut milk, and rum, and beat until incorporated. Add the remaining flour mixture and mix. Stir in the dried cranberries.

4 Spoon the batter into the liners. Bake for 20 minutes, until a toothpick inserted into a cupcake comes out clean. Cool in the pan for 1–2 minutes, then transfer to a wire rack to cool completely.

5 For the frosting, put the egg whites and sugar in the top of a double boiler (or use a heatproof bowl set over a saucepan of gently simmering water) and whisk over simmering water until the sugar has completely dissolved. Remove from the heat and whisk for 4–5 minutes. Add the butter, 2 tablespoons at a time, and beat until it holds stiff peaks. Add the rum and coconut extract and beat until just combined. Spoon the frosting into a pastry bag fitted with a star-shape tip. Pipe onto the cupcakes.

6 To decorate, combine the coconut with a few drops of the food coloring and mix until the color is evenly distributed. Sprinkle over the frosted cupcakes, and insert a cocktail straw into each.

Miami Beach

INGREDIENTS
serves 1
1¾ ounces Scotch whisky
1¼ ounces dry vermouth
1¾ ounces pink grapefruit juice
orange peel strip, to decorate

METHOD

1 Put cracked ice into a cocktail shaker.

2 Pour the whisky, vermouth, and grapefruit juice over the ice.

3 Shake vigorously until well frosted. Strain into a chilled cocktail glass.

4 Decorate with the orange peel strip.

Club Mojito

INGREDIENTS
serves 1

1 teaspoon sugar syrup
6 fresh mint leaves, plus extra
    to decorate
juice of ½ lime
1¾ ounces Jamaican rum
club soda
dash Angostura bitters

METHOD

1 Put the sugar syrup, mint leaves, and lime juice into an old-fashioned glass.

2 Lightly crush the mint leaves, then fill the glass halfway with cracked ice and pour the rum over it.

3 Fill up with club soda.

4 Finish with the Angostura bitters and decorate with the remaining mint leaves.

Coconut & Pineapple Macarons

INGREDIENTS
makes 16

½ cup ground almonds
  (almond meal)
¼ cup finely ground
  unsweetened coconut,
  plus 2 tablespoons toasted,
  to decorate
1 cup confectioners' sugar
2 extra-large egg whites
¼ cup superfine sugar

filling

4 tablespoons unsalted butter,
  softened
2 teaspoons pineapple juice
1 cup confectioners' sugar, sifted
2 slices canned pineapple,
  drained and finely chopped

METHOD

1 Put the ground almonds, ground coconut, and confectioners' sugar into a food processor and process for 15 seconds. Sift the mixture into a bowl. Line two baking sheets with parchment paper.

2 Put the egg whites into a large bowl and whip until holding soft peaks. Gradually beat in the superfine sugar until you have a firm, glossy meringue.

3 Using a spatula, fold the almond mixture into the meringue one-third at a time. When all the dry ingredients are thoroughly incorporated, continue to cut and fold the mixture until it forms a shiny batter with a thick, ribbonlike consistency.

4 Pour the batter into a pastry bag fitted with a ½-inch plain tip. Pipe 32 small circles onto the prepared baking sheets. Tap the baking sheets firmly onto a work surface to remove air bubbles. Sprinkle over the toasted coconut. Let stand at room temperature for 30 minutes. Preheat the oven to 325°F.

5 Bake in the preheated oven for 10–15 minutes. Let cool for 10 minutes. Carefully peel the macarons off the parchment paper and let cool completely.

6 To make the filling, beat the butter and pineapple juice in a bowl until pale and fluffy. Gradually beat in the confectioners' sugar until smooth and creamy, then fold in the chopped pineapple. Use to sandwich pairs of macarons together.

Sex on the Beach

INGREDIENTS
serves 1
¾ ounce peach schnapps
¾ ounce vodka
1¾ ounces fresh orange juice
2½ ounces cranberry and
    peach juice
dash lemon juice
orange peel twist, to decorate

METHOD
1 Pour the liquid ingredients,
except the lemon juice, over
the ice. Shake vigorously until
well frosted.

2 Strain into a glass filled with
crushed ice and splash the
lemon juice over the top.

3 Dress with the orange peel.

46

Mai Tai

INGREDIENTS
serves 1

1¾ ounces white rum
1¾ ounces dark rum
¾ ounce orange curaçao
¾ ounce lime juice
1 tablespoon orgeat syrup
1 tablespoon grenadine
pineapple wedges, cocktail
    cherries, and thinly pared
    orange peel, to decorate

METHOD

1 Put cracked ice into a
cocktail shaker. Pour the
liquid ingredients over the
ice. Shake vigorously until
well frosted.

2 Strain into a chilled cocktail
glass and dress with
pineapple wedges, cocktail
cherries, and orange peel.

Fabulous Food for Friends

Having a glamorous gathering for your friends can be as simple as baking up a batch of cupcakes and giving the old cocktail shaker a shake. Pick a theme and let your food and beverage pairing follow suit.

For holiday parties go for a Strawberrini paired with Chocolate & Pink Peppercorn Cupcakes. Celebrate your best friend's birthday with an indulgent chocolate theme—Chocolate Diva paired with Chili Chocolate Cupcakes. Pina Colada served with Pina Colada Cupcakes are perfect for a pool party, barbecue, or a summer evening get-together. If you're looking to create a refreshing and rejuvenating atmosphere, host a "spa day" and serve nonalcoholic cucumber refreshers with antioxidant-rich green tea along with pomegranate cupcakes.

Happiness is a frosted cupcake with a cherry on top!

Pink Lemon Meringue Cupcakes

INGREDIENTS
makes 12

1½ cups all-purpose flour
1½ teaspoons baking powder
¼ teaspoon salt
1 stick unsalted butter, softened
1 cup superfine sugar or
  granulated sugar
1 teaspoon vanilla extract
2 extra-large eggs
finely grated zest and juice
  of 1 lemon
¼ cup milk
pink food coloring

filling

1 cup lemon curd
½ cup heavy cream, whipped

frosting

4 extra-large egg whites
1 cup superfine sugar or
  granulated sugar
¼ teaspoon cream of tartar
1 tablespoon lemon juice
1 teaspoon lemon extract
pink food coloring, optional

METHOD

1 Preheat the oven to 350°F and line a 12-cup cupcake pan with paper liners.

2 Sift together the flour, baking powder, and salt in a bowl. Put the butter and sugar into a separate bowl and beat until pale and fluffy. Add the vanilla extract, then add the eggs, one at a time, beating after each addition. Add half of the flour mixture, the lemon zest and juice, and milk, and beat until combined. Add the remaining flour mixture and mix. Add a few drops of food coloring and stir until evenly incorporated.

3 Spoon the batter into the paper liners and bake in the preheated oven for 20 minutes, until a toothpick inserted into the center of a cupcake comes out clean. Let cool in the pan for 1–2 minutes, then transfer to a wire rack to cool completely.

4 To make the filling, gently fold the lemon curd into the whipped cream and chill until ready to use.

5 Use an apple corer to remove the center of each cupcake. Spoon the lemon curd filling into the holes.

6 To make the frosting, put the egg whites, sugar, and cream of tartar in the top of a double boiler (or use a heatproof bowl set over a saucepan of gently simmering water) and whisk over simmering water until the sugar has completely dissolved. Remove from the heat and whisk the mixture for 4–5 minutes, until it holds stiff peaks. Add the lemon juice, lemon extract, and a few drops of food coloring, if using, and beat until combined.

7 Spoon the frosting into a pastry bag fitted with a large round tip and pipe onto the cupcakes.

Strawberrini

INGREDIENTS
serves 1
6 fresh or frozen strawberries
1 tablespoon confectioners'
    sugar
splash lime juice
splash fraise liqueur
1¾ ounces vodka, well iced

METHOD
1 Reserve one or two strawberries to add later.

2 Crush the remaining strawberries in a bowl with the sugar, lime juice, and fraise liqueur. Strain well.

3 Pour the vodka into a chilled martini glass and add the puree. Dress with the reserved strawberries.

Woo Woo

INGREDIENTS
serves 1
3½ ounces cranberry juice
1¾ ounces vodka
1¾ ounces peach schnapps

METHOD
1 Fill a chilled cocktail glass halfway with crushed ice.

2 Pour the cranberry juice over the ice.

3 Add the vodka and peach schnapps.

Chocolate & Pink Peppercorn Cupcakes

INGREDIENTS
makes 12

1 cup all-purpose flour
¾ cup unsweetened cocoa
    powder
1 teaspoon baking powder
¼ teaspoon salt
1 stick unsalted butter, softened
1 cup superfine sugar or
    granulated sugar
2 teaspoons vanilla extract
2 extra-large eggs
½ cup sour cream
1 tablespoon pink peppercorns,
    crushed, to decorate

frosting
¼ cup milk
1 tablespoon pink peppercorns,
    crushed
1 stick unsalted butter, softened
2–2 ½ cups confectioners' sugar
    (see method)
2 teaspoons vanilla extract

METHOD

1 Preheat the oven to 350°F and line a 12-cup cupcake pan with paper liners.

2 Sift together the flour, cocoa powder, baking powder, and salt in a bowl. Put the butter and sugar into a separate bowl and beat until pale and fluffy. Add the vanilla extract, then add the eggs, one at a time, beating after each addition. Add half of the flour mixture and the sour cream and beat until combined. Add the remaining flour mixture and mix.

3 Spoon the batter into the paper liners and bake in the preheated oven for 20 minutes, until a toothpick inserted into the center of a cupcake comes out clean. Let cool in the pan for 1–2 minutes, then transfer to a wire rack to cool completely.

4 To make the frosting, put the milk and peppercorns into a small saucepan and heat over medium heat until just boiling. Reduce the heat to low and simmer for about 5 minutes, stirring frequently. Strain the milk into a bowl, discarding the peppercorns, and let cool for about 10 minutes.

5 Add the butter, 2 cups of the confectioners' sugar, and the vanilla extract to the milk and beat, using an electric mixer, until well combined. Add more confectioners' sugar, if needed, to achieve a piping consistency. Spoon the frosting into a pastry bag fitted with a star-shape tip and pipe onto the cupcakes.

6 To decorate, sprinkle the crushed pink peppercorns over the tops of the cupcakes.

Piña Colada

INGREDIENTS
serves 1
1¾ ounces white rum
¾ ounce dark rum
2½ ounces pineapple juice
1¾ ounces cream of coconut
pineapple wedges, to decorate

METHOD
1 Put crushed ice into a
blender with the white rum,
dark rum, pineapple juice,
and cream of coconut
until smooth.

2 Pour, without straining, into
a chilled tall glass and dress
with the pineapple wedges.

Strawberry Colada

INGREDIENTS
serves 1
2½ ounces golden rum
3½ ounces pineapple juice
¾ ounce cream of coconut
6 strawberries, hulled
pineapple wedge, and halved
    strawberry, to decorate

METHOD
1 Put crushed ice into a
blender with the rum,
pineapple juice, and
cream of coconut.

2 Add the strawberries to the
blender. Blend until smooth.

3 Pour, without straining, into
a tall, chilled glass. Decorate
with the pineapple wedge
and halved strawberry.

Pina Colada Cupcakes

INGREDIENTS
makes 12

1½ cups all-purpose flour
1½ teaspoons baking powder
¼ teaspoon salt
1 stick unsalted
 butter, softened
1 cup superfine sugar or
 granulated sugar
2 extra-large eggs
2 tablespoons white rum
½ cup milk
 ½ cup drained, crushed
 canned pineapple (in juice)
¾ cup unsweetened shredded
 dried coconut
12 cocktail umbrellas,
 to decorate

frosting

4 extra-large egg whites
1 cup superfine sugar or
 granulated sugar
¼ teaspoon cream of tartar
1 tablespoon coconut extract
2 tablespoons heavy cream

METHOD

1 Preheat the oven to 350°F. Line a 12-cup cupcake pan with paper liners.

2 Sift together the flour, baking powder, and salt in a bowl. Put the butter and sugar into a separate bowl and beat until pale and fluffy. Add the eggs, one at a time, beating after each addition. Add the rum, milk, and half of the flour mixture and mix until combined. Add the remaining flour mixture and mix thoroughly. Stir in the pineapple.

3 Spoon the batter into the paper liners and bake in the preheated oven for 20 minutes, until a toothpick inserted into the center of a cupcake comes out clean. Let cool in the pan for 1–2 minutes, then transfer to a wire rack to cool completely. Keep the oven on.

4 To toast the coconut, line a baking sheet with aluminum foil and spread the coconut out on it. Bake, tossing halfway through, for about 6–8 minutes, until golden brown. Remove from the oven and let cool.

5 To make the frosting, put the egg whites, sugar, and cream of tartar in the top of a double boiler (or use a heatproof bowl set over a saucepan of gently simmering water) and whisk over simmering water until the sugar has completely dissolved. Remove from the heat and whisk the mixture for 4–5 minutes, or until it holds stiff peaks. Add the coconut extract and heavy cream and stir until just combined. Spoon the frosting into a pastry bag fitted with a star-shape tip and pipe onto the cupcakes.

6 Sprinkle with the toasted coconut and decorate each cupcake with a cocktail umbrella.

Tips for baking success!

CHOOSING INGREDIENTS

Only the most basic ingredients, available at your regular supermarket, are needed to make fantastic cupcakes. Because cupcakes rely on so few ingredients, it's a good idea to splurge for the best quality you can find. From butter (we use unsalted) and eggs to flour (our recipes call for all-purpose) and sugar (for cake batter, look for superfine sugar, or use an equal amount of granulated sugar processed in a food processor for 1 minute, but you could subsitute with granulated sugar), every ingredient is best when you purchase it fresh and of the highest quality.

GETTING STARTED

For the best results, butter, eggs, milk, cream, and other refrigerated ingredients should be brought to room temperature before baking. This helps to make sure your cakes have a tender texture.

MEASURING

Measure liquids in a liquid measuring cup at eye level. To measure dry ingredients in measuring cups or spoons, scoop the ingredient with the measuring cup or spoon and level it off with the flat edge of a blunt knife.

MIXING

Mixing may seem like a no-brainer, but there is a technique to it. Butter and sugar should be well creamed together. This takes about 3 minutes using an electric mixer set on medium speed. Keep creaming until the mixture is light and fluffy. Once the eggs and flour have been added, however, mix only as long as necessary to completely incorporate them without overworking your batter. Be sure, too, to scrape down the bottom and sides of the mixing bowl with a rubber spatula frequently between additions to make sure that all of the ingredients are well mixed.

BAKING AND FROSTING

Always preheat the oven for at least 15 minutes. Scoop your batter into a cupcake pan lined with paper liners. Fill each cup about two-thirds full to produce a nice, dome-shape cupcake that will provide the perfect blank slate for decorating. Avoid overcooking your cupcakes by checking for doneness a minute or two before the recommended cooking time is up. A wooden toothpick inserted into the center of a cupcake should come out clean. When finished, remove from the oven promptly and let the cupcakes cool in the pan for just a minute or two, until they are cool enough to handle. Using a spatula or small knife, lift the cupcakes (in their paper liners) from the pan and transfer to a wire rack to cool completely.

Always cool cupcakes completely before frosting. Once they're cooled, it's time to get artsy with the frosting, sprinkles, and other decorations. Have fun decorating your little cakes and you'll set the tone for a fun-filled party.

Skinny Strawberry Fizz Cocktail

INGREDIENTS
serves 4

8 ounces strawberries, hulled
1 ounce agave syrup
juice of 1 lime
3½ ounces vodka
diet cola
whole strawberries and lime peel
   twists, to decorate

METHOD

1 Put the strawberries, syrup, and lime juice in a plastic pitcher and process with an immersion blender or in a food processor until smooth.

2 Add crushed ice to each of four tall glasses.

3 Pour the strawberry mixture evenly into each glass, divide the vodka between the glasses, and stir to mix.

4 Fill up the glasses with the cola to taste, place a strawberry and lime peel twist on the rims.

Skinny Apricot Refresher

INGREDIENTS

serves 2

6 apricots
1 orange
1 fresh lemongrass stalk
¾-inch piece fresh ginger,
    peeled

METHOD

1 Halve and pit the apricots.
Peel the orange, leaving
some of the white pith. Cut
the lemongrass into chunks.

2 Place the apricots, orange,
lemongrass, and ginger in a
juicer and juice together all
the ingredients. Pour the mixture
into glasses, add ice cubes,
and serve.

Who says treats have to be indulgent!

Skinny Mini Muffins

INGREDIENTS
makes 48

1½ cups all-purpose flour
1 tablespoon baking powder
⅓ cup firmly packed light
   brown sugar
¾ cup dried cranberries
½ cup miniature marshmallows
finely grated rind of
   ½ small lemon
1 tablespoon lemon juice
1 egg, beaten
½ cup skim milk
3 tablespoons sunflower oil
½ teaspoon vanilla extract

METHOD

1 Preheat the oven to 400°F.
Put 48 paper cupcake liners
on two or three baking
sheets or in cupcake pans.

2 Sift the flour and baking
powder into a bowl and add
the sugar. Stir in the
cranberries and
marshmallows.

3 Whisk together lemon rind
and juice, egg, milk, oil, and
vanilla in a bowl, then stir into
the dry ingredients to make
a soft batter.

4 Spoon the batter into
the paper liners and bake
in the preheated oven for
12–15 minutes, or until risen,
firm, and golden. Transfer
to a wire rack to cool
before serving.

Watermelon Cupcakes

INGREDIENTS
makes 12

1½ cups all-purpose flour
1½ teaspoons baking powder
¼ teaspoon salt
1 stick unsalted butter, softened
1 cup superfine sugar or
   granulated sugar
2 teaspoons vanilla extract
2 extra-large eggs
½ cup milk
pink food coloring
½ cup mini semisweet
   chocolate chips

frosting

1 stick unsalted butter, softened
2–2½ cups confectioners' sugar
   (see method)
1 tablepoon milk
1 teaspoon vanilla extract
pinch of salt
green food coloring

METHOD

1 Preheat the oven to 350°F and line a 12-cup cupcake pan with paper liners.

2 Sift together the flour, baking powder, and salt in a bowl. Put the butter and sugar into a separate bowl and beat until pale and fluffy. Add the vanilla extract, then add the eggs, one at a time, beating after each addition. Add half of the flour mixture and the milk and beat until incorporated. Add the remaining flour mixture and mix. Add several drops of food coloring and beat until evenly combined. Gradually add more coloring until a vibrant pink is achieved. Stir in the chocolate chips.

3 Spoon the batter into the paper liners and bake in the preheated oven for 20 minutes, until a toothpick inserted into the center of a cupcake comes out clean. Let cool in the pan for 1–2 minutes, then transfer to a wire rack to cool completely.

4 To make the frosting, put the butter, 2 cups of the confectioners' sugar, the milk, vanilla extract, and salt into a bowl and beat with an electric mixer until well combined. Add more confectioners' sugar, if needed, to achieve a piping consistency. Add several drops of food coloring and beat until evenly incorporated. Gradually add more coloring until a dark green color is achieved. Transfer the frosting to a pastry bag fitted with a star-shape tip and pipe onto the cupcakes.

Cucumber Refresher

INGREDIENTS
serves 1
2–3 fresh mint sprigs
1 teaspoon confectioners' sugar
juice 1 lime
1-inch piece cucumber,
    thinly sliced
sparkling water, chilled

METHOD
1 Remove the leaves from the mint sprigs and chop finely. Mix half of the chopped mint with the sugar on a saucer.

2 Rub a little of the lime juice around the rim of a wine glass and dip in the minted sugar to frost.

3 Put the remaining lime juice and chopped mint into the prepared glass with the cucumber and cracked ice. Fill up with chilled sparkling water.

Rum Cooler

INGREDIENTS
serves 1
1¼ ounces white rum
1¼ ounces pineapple juice
1 banana, peeled and sliced
juice of 1 lime
lime peel twist, to decorate

METHOD

1 Put ice, rum, pineapple juice, and banana into a blender.

2 Add the lime juice and blend for about 1 minute, or until smooth.

3 Fill a chilled glass with cracked ice and pour the cocktail over the ice.

4 Decorate with the lime peel.

Pomegranate & Green Tea Cupcakes

INGREDIENTS
makes 12

1½ cups all-purpose flour
1½ teaspoons baking powder
1 tablespoon green tea
　(matcha) powder
¼ teaspoon salt
1 stick unsalted butter, softened
1 cup superfine sugar or
　granulated sugar
1 teaspoon vanilla extract
2 extra-large eggs
¼ cup milk
¼ cup pomegranate seeds,
　to decorate

pomegranate syrup

2 cups pomegranate juice
½ cup superfine sugar or
　granulated sugar

frosting

1 stick unsalted butter, softened
1½–2 cups confectioners' sugar
　(see method)

METHOD

1 To make the pomegranate syrup, put the pomegranate juice and sugar into a saucepan and bring to a boil over medium–high heat, stirring occasionally, until the sugar has dissolved. Reduce the heat to low and cook until the mixture has reduced to about ½ cup. Set aside to cool.

2 Preheat the oven to 350°F. Line a 12-cup cupcake pan with paper liners.

3 Sift together the flour, baking powder, green tea powder, and salt in a bowl. Put the butter and sugar into a separate bowl and beat until pale and fluffy. Add the vanilla extract, then add the eggs, one at a time, beating after each addition. Add half of the flour mixture, ¼ cup of the pomegranate syrup, and the milk and mix to incorporate. Add the remaining flour mixture and mix.

4 Spoon the batter into the paper liners and bake in the preheated oven for 20 minutes, or until a toothpick inserted into the center of a cupcake comes out clean. Let cool in the pan for 1–2 minutes, then transfer to a wire rack to cool completely.

5 To make the frosting, put the butter, 1½ cups confectioners' sugar, and remaining pomegranate syrup in a bowl and beat with an electric mixer until well combined. Add more confectioners' sugar, if needed, to achieve a piping consistency. Spoon the frosting into a pastry bag fitted with a star-shape tip and pipe onto the cupcakes.

6 To decorate, sprinkle the pomegranate seeds over the cupcakes.

Vanilla Chai Tea Cupcakes

INGREDIENTS
makes 12

½ cup milk
3 chai tea bags
1½ cups all-purpose flour
1½ teaspoons baking powder
1 teaspoon pumpkin pie spice
¼ teaspoon salt
1 stick unsalted butter, softened
1 cup superfine sugar or
    granulated sugar
1 tablespoon vanilla extract
2 extra-large eggs
1 teaspoon ground cinnamon
    and 1 tablespoon sugar,
    mixed, to decorate

frosting

3 extra-large egg whites
¾ cup superfine sugar or
    granulated sugar
2 sticks unsalted butter, softened
1 teaspoon vanilla extract
1 teaspoon ground cinnamon

METHOD

1 Preheat the oven to 350°F and line a 12-cup cupcake pan with paper liners.

2 Heat the milk in a small saucepan until just boiling. Add the tea bags, remove from the heat, and let steep for 15 minutes. Remove and discard the tea bags and set the milk aside to cool completely.

3 Sift together the flour, baking powder, pumpkin pie spice, and salt in a bowl. Put the butter and sugar into a separate bowl and beat until pale and fluffy. Add the vanilla extract, then add the eggs, one at a time, beating after each addition, until combined. Add half of the flour mixture and the tea-steeped milk and beat until combined. Add the remaining flour and mix.

4 Spoon the batter into the paper liners and bake in the preheated oven for 20 minutes, until a toothpick inserted into the center of a cupcake comes out clean. Remove from the oven, let cool in the pan for 1–2 minutes, then transfer to a wire rack to cool completely.

5 To make the frosting, put the egg whites and sugar in the top of a double boiler (or use a heatproof bowl set over a saucepan of gently simmering water) and whisk over simmering water until the sugar has completely dissolved. Remove from the heat and whisk for 4–5 minutes. Add the butter, 2 tablespoons at a time, and beat until it holds stiff peaks. Add the vanilla extract and cinnamon and beat until just combined. Spoon the frosting into a pastry bag fitted with a star-shape tip and pipe onto the cupcakes.

6 To decorate, sprinkle the cinnamon sugar over the top of the cupcakes.

With chocolate and friends, you can conquer just about anything!

Devil's Food Chocolate Cupcakes

INGREDIENTS
makes 18
4 tablespoons soft margarine
½ cup brown sugar
2 extra-large eggs
¾ cup all-purpose flour
½ teaspoon baking soda
¼ cup unsweetened cocoa
   powder
½ cup sour cream

frosting
4 ounces semisweet chocolate,
   broken into pieces
2 tablespoons superfine sugar or
   granulated sugar
⅔ cup sour cream
shaved chocolate curls,
   to decorate

METHOD
1 Preheat the oven to 350°F and line an 18-cup cupcake pan with paper liners.

2 Put the margarine, brown sugar, eggs, flour, baking soda, and cocoa in a large bowl and, using an electric handheld mixer, beat together until just smooth. Using a metal spoon, fold in the sour cream. Divide the batter equally among the paper liners and smooth the tops.

3 Bake in the preheated oven for 20 minutes, or until well risen and firm to the touch. Transfer to a wire rack to cool.

4 To make the frosting, melt the chocolate in the top of a double boiler (or use a heatproof bowl set over a saucepan of gently simmering water). Cool slightly, then beat in the sugar and sour cream until combined. Spread the frosting over each cake and let set in the refrigerator. Serve decorated with chocolate curls.

Chocolate Martini

INGREDIENTS
serves 1

lemon wedge
unsweetened cocoa powder
1¾ ounces vodka
¼ ounce crème de cacao
2 dashes orange flower water

METHOD

1 Rub the rim of a chilled cocktail glass with the lemon wedge, then dip in a saucer of cocoa powder.

2 Put cracked ice into a cocktail shaker. Pour the vodka, crème de cacao, and orange flower water over the ice. Shake vigorously until well frosted.

3 Strain into the glass.

Chocolate Diva

INGREDIENTS

serves 1

4 squares good-quality milk
   chocolate, melted
¾ ounce vodka
¾ ounce Grand Marnier
¾ ounce crème de cacao
½ ounce fresh orange juice
fresh edible petals, to decorate

METHOD

1 Mix the melted chocolate
gently with the vodka, liqueurs,
and the orange juice until
well blended.

2 Pour into a chilled cocktail
glass and float petals on the
top to decorate.

Chili Chocolate Cupcakes

INGREDIENTS
makes 12
1 cup all-purpose flour
¾ cup unsweetened cocoa
    powder
1½ teaspoons baking powder
½ teaspoon ground cinnamon
1 teaspoon mild chili powder
¼ teaspoon cayenne pepper
¼ teaspoon salt
1 stick unsalted butter, softened
1 cup superfine sugar or
    granulated sugar
2 teaspoons vanilla extract
2 extra-large eggs
½ cup milk
2 ounces semisweet chocolate,
    to decorate

frosting
1 stick unsalted butter, softened
1½–2 cups confectioners' sugar
    (see method)
¼ cup unsweetened cocoa
    powder
2 tablespoons milk
1 teaspoon vanilla extract
1 teaspoon ground cinnamon

METHOD
1 Preheat the oven to 350°F and line a 12-cup cupcake pan with paper liners.

2 Sift together the flour, cocoa powder, baking powder, cinnamon, chili powder, cayenne pepper, and salt in a bowl. Put the butter and sugar into a separate bowl and beat until pale and fluffy. Add the vanilla extract, then add the eggs, one at a time, beating after each addition. Add half of the flour mixture and the milk and beat until incorporated. Add the remaining flour mixture and mix.

3 Spoon the batter into the paper liners and bake in the preheated oven for 20 minutes, until risen and a toothpick inserted into the center of a cupcake comes out clean. Let cool in the pan for 1–2 minutes, then transfer to a wire rack to cool completely.

4 To make the frosting, put the butter in a bowl and beat with an electric mixer until pale and fluffy. Add 1½ cups of the confectioners' sugar together with the cocoa powder, milk, vanilla extract, and cinnamon. Beat together until well combined. Add more confectioners' sugar, if necessary, to achieve a piping consistency. Spoon the frosting into a pastry bag fitted with a star-shape tip and pipe onto the cupcakes.

5 To decorate, grate the chocolate over the top of the cupcakes.

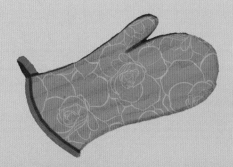

Salted Caramel Cupcakes

INGREDIENTS
makes 12

1½ cups all-purpose flour
1½ teaspoons baking powder
¼ teaspoon salt
1 stick unsalted butter, softened
½ cup superfine sugar or
    granulated sugar
½ cup firmly packed dark
    brown sugar
1 teaspoon vanilla extract
1 teaspoon coffee extract
2 extra-large eggs
½ cup milk
1 teaspoon sea salt flakes,
    to decorate

frosting

1 stick unsalted butter, softened
1 cup firmly packed dark
    brown sugar
⅓ cup heavy cream
½ teaspoon salt
1½–2½ cups confectioners'
    sugar (see method)

METHOD

1 Preheat the oven to 350°F and line a 12-cup cupcake pan with paper liners.

2 Sift together the flour, baking powder, and salt in a bowl. Put the butter, sugar, and brown sugar into a separate bowl and cream until fluffy. Add the vanilla extract and coffee extract, then add the eggs one at a time, beating after each addition. Add half of the flour mixture and the milk and beat until incorporated. Add the remaining flour mixture and mix well.

3 Spoon the batter into the paper liners and bake in the preheated oven for 20 minutes, until a toothpick inserted into the center of a cupcake comes out clean. Let cool in the pan for 1–2 minutes, then transfer to a wire rack to cool completely.

4 To make the frosting, first prepare a caramel sauce by melting the butter in a small saucepan over medium heat. Add the brown sugar, cream, and salt and cook, stirring continuously, for about 4 minutes, or until the sugar has completely dissolved. Remove from the heat and set aside to cool.

5 Add 1½ cups of the confectioners' sugar to the caramel sauce and beat until fully incorporated. Add more confectioners' sugar, if needed, to achieve a piping consistency. Spoon into a pastry bag fitted with a star-shape tip and pipe onto the cupcakes.

6 To decorate, sprinkle the cupcakes with sea salt flakes.

Vanilla Swirl Brownies

INGREDIENTS
makes 12

6 tablespoons lightly salted
    butter, plus extra for greasing
4 ounces semisweet
    chocolate, coarsely chopped
1 egg
1 egg yolk

½ cup firmly packed light
    brown sugar
⅓ cup all-purpose flour
½ teaspoon baking powder
3 ounces milk chocolate,
    coarsely chopped

frosting

⅔ cup mascarpone cheese
¼ cup confectioners' sugar
1 teaspoon vanilla extract
milk or semisweet chocolate
    curls, to sprinkle

METHOD

1 Preheat the oven to 375°F and grease a 12-cup cupcake pan.

2 Put the butter and semisweet chocolate into the top of a double boiler (or use a heatproof bowl set over a saucepan of gently simmering water) and heat until melted. Let the mixture stand to cool slightly.

3 Put the egg, egg yolk, and light brown sugar in a mixing bowl and beat together with an electric handheld mixer until the batter begins to turn frothy. Stir in the melted chocolate. Sift the flour and baking powder into the bowl, sprinkle in the milk chocolate, and stir together. Using a teaspoon, spoon the batter into the prepared cupcake pan.

4 Bake in the preheated oven for 12–15 minutes, or until the brownies feel dry but give a little when gently pressed. (If you're unsure, it's better to slightly undercook brownies because they lose their gooeyness when overbaked.) Let stand in the pan for 10 minutes, then transfer to a wire rack to cool.

5 For the frosting, put the mascarpone cheese, confectioners' sugar, and vanilla in a small bowl and beat with an electric handheld mixer until smooth and creamy. Put the mixture in a pastry bag fitted with a ½-inch star-shape tip and pipe swirls over the cakes. Sprinkle with chocolate curls to decorate.

Celebrate in Style

There is nothing like a tower of beautifully decorated cupcakes or a tray of expertly mixed cocktails to mark a special occasion. Put them together and you are all set to celebrate in style. Whether feting an engagement, a special anniversary, or an important achievement, the perfect cupcake-and-cocktail pairing is sure to strike just the right note.

Both cupcakes and cocktails offer opportunities for endless creativity. Mixing and matching both flavors and visual elements is key to letting them shine. Pairing them in clever ways only adds to their power to delight.

In their simplest forms, both cupcakes and cocktails set a celebratory tone, but served in fancy glasses rimmed with sparkling decorating sugar or adorned with glittering sprinkles, heart-shape decorations, or candy canes and reindeer, they take your celebration to the next level and create an unbeatable ambience all on their own.

Champagne Cocktail

INGREDIENTS
serves 1
1 sugar cube
2 dashes Angostura bitters
¾ ounce brandy
champagne, chilled

METHOD
1 Place the sugar cube
in the bottom of a chilled
champagne flute with
the Angostura bitters.

2 Pour over the brandy
and fill up slowly with
champagne.

Bellini

INGREDIENTS
serves 1
1 lemon wedge
superfine sugar
¾ ounce peach juice
2½ ounces champagne, chilled

METHOD
1 Rub the rim of a chilled champagne flute with the lemon wedge, then dip in a saucer of sugar to frost.

2 Pour the peach juice into the prepared glass.

3 Add the chilled champagne.

Strawberry Mimosa Cupcakes

INGREDIENTS
makes 12

1½ cups all-purpose flour
1½ teaspoons baking powder
¼ teaspoon salt
1 stick unsalted butter, softened
1 cup superfine sugar or
  granulated sugar
1 teaspoon vanilla extract
2 eggs
½ cup champagne or other
  sparkling wine
finely grated zest of 1 orange
2 tablespoons orange juice

filling

¼ cup water
2 tablespoons cornstarch
1 cup hulled, diced fresh or
  frozen strawberries
⅓ cup granulated sugar
¼ cup champagne or other
  sparkling wine

frosting

1 stick unsalted butter, softened
3½–4 cups confectioners' sugar
  (see method)
¼ cup champagne, or other
  sparkling wine
finely grated zest of 1 orange
2 tablespoons orange juice

to decorate

4 ounces marzipan
red food coloring
yellow food coloring
orange edible-ink marker
pink sugar crystals

METHOD

1 Preheat the oven to 350°F and line a 12-cup cupcake pan with paper liners.

2 Sift together the flour, baking powder, and salt in a bowl. Put the butter and sugar into a separate bowl and beat until pale and fluffy. Add the vanilla extract, then add the eggs, one at a time, beating after each addition. Add half of the flour mixture and the champagne and beat until combined. Add the remaining flour mixture, the orange zest, and orange juice and mix.

3 Spoon the batter into the paper liners and bake in the preheated oven for 20 minutes, until a toothpick inserted into the center of a cupcake comes out clean. Let cool in the pan for 1–2 minutes, then transfer to a wire rack to cool completely.

4 To make the filling, stir the water and cornstarch in a saucepan and bring to a boil over medium–high heat, stirring. Add the strawberries and sugar, reduce the heat to low, and simmer, stirring frequently, for 5 minutes, until the mixture has thickened. Add the champagne and continue to simmer for an additional 3–5 minutes, until the mixture has thickened. Set aside to cool.

5 To make the frosting, put the butter, 3½ cups of the confectioners' sugar, champagne, orange zest, and orange juice into a bowl and beat with an electric mixer until well combined. Add more confectioners' sugar, if necessary, to achieve a piping consistency. Spoon into a pastry bag fitted with a star-shape tip.

6 To make the orange wedge decorations, divide the marzipan in half. Add a few drops of red food coloring and a few drops of yellow food coloring to one half of the marzipan and knead until evenly incorporated. Add more red color, if needed, to achieve a dark orange color; this will be used to make the orange rind. Add a couple of drops of yellow food coloring and a couple of drops of red food coloring to the

and knead until evenly incorporated; this will be used to make the inside of the wedges in a lighter orange color.

7 Divide both marzipan colors into 12 pieces. Take one piece of light orange marzipan and shape into a semicircle about ¼ inch thick. Lightly pinch the flat side of the semicircle to make a wedge shape. Flatten a piece of the dark orange marzipan and press in place around the curved edge of the light orange wedge, trimming as necessary to give the effect of a peel. Repeat with the remaining marzipan to make 12 orange wedges in total. Using the edible-ink marker, draw lines on the lighter orange part to represent the inner membrane of an orange wedge. Set aside to dry.

8 Use an apple corer to remove the center of each cupcake. Spoon the strawberry filling into the holes. Pipe the frosting onto the cupcakes, sprinkle with sugar crystals, then top each cupcake with a marzipan orange wedge.

Mimosa

INGREDIENTS
serves 1
1 passion fruit
½ ounce orange curaçao
champagne, chilled
star fruit (carambola) slice,
    to decorate

METHOD
1 Scoop out the passion fruit
flesh into a shaker and shake
with the curaçao and
cracked ice until frosted.

2 Pour into a chilled
champagne flute and
top up with champagne.

3 Dress with the star fruit slice.

Maidenly Mimosa

INGREDIENTS
serves 2
6 ounces orange juice
6 ounces sparkling white
    grape juice

METHOD

1 Chill two champagne
flutes.

2 Divide the orange juice
between the flutes.

3 Fill up with the sparkling
grape juice.

Vanilla Rose Macarons

INGREDIENTS
makes 16

¾ cup ground almonds
(almond meal)
1 cup confectioners' sugar
2 extra-large egg whites
¼ cup superfine sugar or
granulated sugar
½ teaspoon vanilla extract

filling

½ stick butter, softened
½ teaspoon rose water
a few drops of pink food
coloring
1 cup confectioners' sugar, sifted
crystalized rose petals, to
decorate (optional)

METHOD

1 Line two baking sheets with parchment paper. Put the ground almonds and confectioners' sugar into a food processor and process for 15 seconds. Sift the mixture into a bowl.

2 Put the egg whites into a large bowl and whisk until holding soft peaks. Gradually beat in the superfine or granulated sugar to make a firm, glossy meringue. Beat in the vanilla extract.

3 Using a spatula, fold the almond mixture into the meringue one-third at a time. When all the dry ingredients are fully incorporated, continue to cut and fold the mixture until it forms a shiny batter with a thick, ribbonlike consistency.

4 Pour the batter into a pastry bag fitted with a ½-inch plain tip. Pipe 32 small circles onto the prepared baking sheets. Tap the baking sheets firmly onto a work surface to remove air bubbles. Let stand at room temperature for 30 minutes. Preheat the oven to 325°F.

5 Bake in the preheated oven for 10–15 minutes. Let cool for 10 minutes. Carefully peel the macarons off the parchment paper and let cool completely.

6 To make the filling, beat the butter, rose water, and pink food coloring in a bowl until pale and fluffy. Gradually beat in the confectioners' sugar until smooth. Use to sandwich together pairs of macarons and decorate with petals, if using.

White Chocolate & Rose Cupcakes

INGREDIENTS
makes 12

1 stick butter, softened,
    or ½ cup soft margarine
½ cup superfine sugar or
    granulated sugar
1 teaspoon rose water
2 eggs, lightly beaten
1 cup all-purpose flour
1 teaspoon baking powder
2 ounces white chocolate,
    grated

frosting

4 ounces white chocolate,
    broken into pieces
2 tablespoons milk
¾ cup cream cheese
¼ cup confectioners' sugar

to decorate

a few pink rose petals
1 egg white, lightly beaten
confectioners' sugar, for dusting

METHOD

1 Preheat the oven to 350°F and line a 12-cup cupcake pan with paper liners.

2 Place the butter, sugar, and rose water in a large bowl and beat together until light and fluffy. Gradually beat in the eggs. Sift in the flour and baking powder and, using a metal spoon, fold in gently. Fold in the grated chocolate.

3 Spoon the batter into the paper liners. Bake in the preheated oven for 15–20 minutes, or until a toothpick inserted into the center of a cupcake comes out clean. Transfer to a wire rack and let cool.

4 To make the frosting, put the chocolate and milk into the top of a double boiler (or use a heatproof bowl set over a saucepan of gently simmering water) and heat until melted. Remove from the heat and stir until smooth. Let cool for 30 minutes. Put the cream cheese in a separate bowl, sift in the confectioners' sugar, and beat together until smooth and creamy. Fold in the melted chocolate. Chill in the refrigerator for 1 hour.

5 Swirl the frosting over the tops of the cupcakes. To decorate, lightly brush the rose petals with a little of the beaten egg white. Sprinkle with sugar and let set. Arrange the sugar-frosted petals on top of the cupcakes.

Wedding Belle

INGREDIENTS
serves 1

1¾ ounces gin
1¾ ounces Dubonnet
¾ ounce cherry brandy
¾ ounce orange juice
orange peel strip, to decorate

METHOD

1 Put cracked ice into a cocktail shaker. Pour the liquid ingredients over the ice. Shake vigorously until well frosted.

2 Strain into a chilled cocktail glass and decorate with the orange peel.

White Diamond Frappe

INGREDIENTS
serves 1
¼ ounce peppermint schnapps
¼ ounce white crème de cacao
¼ ounce anise liqueur
¼ ounce lemon juice

METHOD

1 Put cracked ice into a cocktail shaker. Pour the ingredients over the ice. Shake vigorously until well frosted.

2 Strain into a chilled shot glass and add a small spoonful of crushed ice.

Champagne is always appropriate for a grand celebration. Whether you're celebrating a graduation, a big promotion at work, or a milestone birthday, sparkling Champagne Cocktails, Mimosas, or Bellinis in gorgeous champagne flutes will mark the occasion in grand fashion.

Likewise, champagne, roses, hearts, and sparkly stuff are all great for setting the tone for love and romance. Champagne Cocktails or Mimosas paired with White Chocolate & Rose Cupcakes are perfectly suited to a midday bridal shower. Pair Kir Royales with Chocolate Meringue Kisses for an engagement party or anniversary celebration. Celebrate a wedding with White Diamond Frappes served with Heart Cupcakes.

Warm beverages and spicy notes set a cozy tone for the winter holidays. Eggnogg served with Chili & Cardamon Chocolate Thins or Mulled Wine paired with Cranberry & Orange Pies are are sure to invoke a holiday spirit. Of course, a Champagne Pick-Me-Up is the perfect foil for a New Year's Day brunch.

Heart-in-a-Cupcake

INGREDIENTS
makes 12

2¼ cups all-purpose flour
2¼ teaspoons baking powder
¼ teaspoon salt
1½ sticks unsalted butter,
    softened, plus extra for
    greasing
1½ cups superfine sugar or
    granulated sugar
1 tablespoon vanilla extract
3 extra-large eggs
1¾ cups milk
pink food coloring
pink gum-paste hearts,
    to decorate

frosting

3 extra-large egg whites
¾ cup superfine sugar or
    granulated sugar
2 sticks unsalted butter, softened
1 teaspoon vanilla extract
pink food coloring

METHOD

1 Preheat the oven to 350°F and grease a 9-inch round cake pan. Draw a straight line down the middle of the bottom (outside) of each of 12 pink or red paper cupcake liners. Put the liners in a 12-cup cupcake pan, with the lines all facing the same direction. Remember which direction the lines are facing because this will show you how to align your hidden hearts.

2 Sift together the flour, baking powder, and salt in a bowl. Put the butter and sugar into a separate bowl and beat until pale and fluffy. Add the vanilla extract, then add the eggs, one at a time, beating after each addition. Add half of the flour mixture and the milk and beat until incorporated. Add the remaining flour mixture and mix.

3 Transfer about one-third of the batter to a separate bowl and mix in several drops of pink food coloring until evenly distributed. Spread the batter evenly in the prepared cake pan and bake in the preheated oven for 18 minutes, or until the cake is just cooked. Let cool in the pan for 1–2 minutes, then turn out onto a wire rack and let cool completely (do not turn off the oven).

4 Use a 1½-inch heart-shape cookie cutter to cut out 12 hearts from the pink cake. Discard the trimmings. Spoon a generous tablespoon of the remaining cake batter into the bottom of one of the paper liners and then stand a heart vertically in the middle, lining it up with the line drawn on the bottom of the liner. Spoon more batter around the sides of the heart until the liner is about two-thirds full. Repeat to fill all 12 liners. Cover the cupcake pan with aluminum foil to prevent the prebaked hearts from drying out.

5 Bake in the preheated oven for 20 minutes, until a toothpick inserted into the center of a cupcake comes out clean. Let cool in the pan for 1–2 minutes, then transfer to a wire rack to cool completely.

6 To make the frosting, put the egg whites and sugar in the top of a double boiler (or use a heatproof bowl set over a saucepan of gently simmering water) and whisk over simmering water until the sugar has completely dissolved. Remove from the heat and whisk the mixture for 4–5 minutes, until it holds stiff peaks. Add the butter, 2 tablespoons at a time, and continue to beat until it holds stiff peaks. Add the vanilla extract and several drops of pink food coloring and beat until the color is fully incorporated. Gradually beat in more food coloring until the desired shade is achieved. Spoon the frosting into a piping bag fitted with a star-shape tip.

7 Pipe the frosting onto the cupcakes and sprinkle with gum-paste hearts. Cut in half to serve so that the hearts will show.

French Kiss

INGREDIENTS
serves 1
1¾ ounces bourbon
¾ ounce apricot liqueur
2 teaspoons grenadine
1 teaspoon lemon juice

METHOD
1 Put cracked ice into a cocktail shaker.

2 Pour the liquid ingredients over the ice.

3 Shake vigorously until well frosted.

4 Strain into a chilled cocktail glass.

Kir Royale

INGREDIENTS
serves 1

a few drops crème de cassis,
    or to taste
½ ounce brandy (optional)
champagne, chilled

METHOD

1 Pour the crème de cassis
and brandy, if using, into a
chilled champagne flute.

2 Wait a moment, and
then gently pour in the
champagne.

Chocolate Meringue Kisses

INGREDIENTS
makes 40

3 egg whites
1 teaspoon raspberry vinegar
¾ cup superfine sugar
1 teaspoon cornstarch
2 tablespoons unsweetened
   cocoa powder, sifted
8 ounces semisweet chocolate,
   coarsely chopped

METHOD

1 Preheat the oven to 325°F. Line three baking sheets with nonstick parchment paper.

2 Whisk the egg whites in a large, clean mixing bowl until you have stiff, moist-looking peaks. Gradually whisk in the vinegar and sugar, a tablespoonful at a time, until thick and glossy. Using a large metal spoon, gently fold in the cornstarch and cocoa powder.

3 Spoon the mixture into a pastry bag fitted with a large star tip and pipe forty 1-inch "kisses" onto the prepared baking sheets.

4 Put the sheets in the preheated oven, then immediately turn the heat down to 250°F. Bake for 45 minutes, or until crisp on the outside. Transfer the meringues to a wire rack, still on the paper, and let cool for 1 hour, then peel off the paper.

5 Meanwhile, put the chocolate into the top of a double boiler (or use a heatproof bowl set over a saucepan of gently simmering water) and heat until melted.

6 Line the baking sheets with more parchment paper. Dip the bottoms of the meringue kisses in the melted chocolate and place them, chocolate side up, on the prepared baking sheets. Let set for 1 hour. Store in an airtight container in a cool, dry place for up to two weeks.

Valentine Berry Love Pies

INGREDIENTS
makes 24 individual pies
a little butter, for greasing
12 ounces strawberries
2 teaspoons cornstarch
2 tablespoons strawberry jelly
    or preserves
grated rind of 2 limes
1 (1-pound) package
    ready-to-bake rolled
    dough pie crust, chilled
a little all-purpose flour,
    for dusting
1 egg yolk mixed with
    1 tablespoon water, to glaze
superfine sugar, for sprinkling

to serve
1 cup heavy cream
grated rind of 2 limes
2 tablespoons confectioners'
    sugar

METHOD
1 Preheat the oven to 350°F and lightly grease two 12-cup cupcake pans.

2 Coarsely chop the strawberries. Put them in a mixing bowl and stir in the cornstarch, jelly or preserves, and lime rind.

3 Roll out half of the pie dough thinly on a lightly floured surface. Using a fluted cookie cutter, stamp out 24 circles, each 2½ inches in diameter. Press these gently into the prepared pans, rerolling the scraps as needed.

4 Brush the top edges of the pastry shells with a little of the egg glaze, then spoon in the filling.

5 Roll the remaining pie dough out thinly on a lightly floured surface. Use a 2-inch heart-shape cookie cutter to cut out 24 hearts. Use the hearts as lids, pressing the edges together. Brush egg glaze over the pastry and sprinkle with superfine sugar.

6 Bake in the preheated oven for 15 minutes, or until golden brown. Let stand to cool in the pans for 10 minutes, then loosen with a blunt knife and transfer to a wire rack to cool.

7 Whip the cream until it forms soft swirls, then fold in half of the lime rind and all of the confectioners' sugar. Sprinkle with the rest of the lime rind. Serve the pies with spoonfuls of whipped cream.

A Sloe Kiss

INGREDIENTS
serves 1
½ ounce sloe gin
½ ounce Southern Comfort
¾ ounce vodka
1 teaspoon amaretto
splash of Galliano
orange juice
orange peel twist, to decorate

METHOD
1 Put cracked ice into a cocktail shaker, pour in the sloe gin, Southern Comfort, vodka, and amaretto, and shake until well frosted.

2 Strain into a long, chilled glass filled with cracked ice.

3 Splash on the Galliano.

4 Fill up with orange juice and decorate with the orange peel.

Purple Passion

INGREDIENTS
serves 1
1¾ ounces vodka
3½ ounces grapefruit juice
3½ ounces purple grape juice

METHOD
1 Fill a chilled highball glass with cracked ice.

2 Put cracked ice into a cocktail shaker. Pour the liquid ingredients over the ice. Shake vigorously until well frosted.

3 Strain into the glass.

For special celebrations and festive holidays, a few pretty garnishes and clever decorating techniques are all you need to make your celebration extra special. Decorate glasses by moistening the rim (we like to use a slit wedge of lemon or lime), then dip the rim in a wide bowl filled with decorating sugar or coarse salt. A wedge or twist of citrus is a lovely finishing touch for most cocktails. Garnish sweet, fruity cocktails with skewers of fruit (pineapple, kiwi, grapes, and berries are colorful and look great), creamy drinks with peppermint sticks, or savory drinks with pickled green beans, olives, celery stalks, or slices of cucumber.

For cupcakes, add heart-shape decorations for romantic occasions, and white or shimmering metallic frosting, flowers, and other decorations for bridal showers and weddings. For the winter holidays, let the whimsy of the season be your guide and decorate cupcakes with snowmen, tiny Santas, wrapped presents, reindeer, holly, and mistletoe.

Holiday Eggnog

INGREDIENTS
makes 8 cups

6 extra-large eggs
½ cup plus 2 tablespoons
  granulated sugar
2 cups half-and-half
2 cups milk

½ cup brandy
¼ cup light rum
1 teaspoon vanilla extract
2 cups heavy cream
freshly grated nutmeg

METHOD

1 Beat the eggs with an electric mixer on medium speed until thick and a lemon color; gradually add ½ cup of the sugar, beating well.

2 Put the half-and-half and milk into a large saucepan over medium–low heat and heat until thoroughly hot but not boiling. Gradually add the hot milk mixture to the egg mixture, stirring with a wire whisk. Transfer the mixture back to the large saucepan and cook over medium–low heat, stirring continuously with a wire whisk until hot but not boiling. Remove from the heat and let cool. Stir in the brandy, rum, and vanilla with a wire whisk. Cover and refrigerate until thoroughly chilled.

3 Just before serving, beat the heavy cream and the remaining 2 tablespoons of sugar in a large bowl until soft peaks form. Pour the chilled eggnog mixture into a large punch bowl. Gently fold the whipped cream into the eggnog mixture just until combined. Decorate each serving with freshly grated nutmeg.

Chili & Cardamom Chocolate Thins

INGREDIENTS
makes 40

Chili Chocolate Thins
8 ounces semisweet chocolate,
   coarsely chopped
a large pinch of hot chili powder
edible glitter, to decorate

Cardamom White Chocolate Thins
8 ounces white chocolate,
   coarsely chopped
½ teaspoon cardamom seeds,
   crushed
3 tablespoons finely chopped
   pistachio nuts, plus extra
   to decorate
edible glitter, to decorate

METHOD

1 Line four baking sheets with nonstick parchment paper.

2 For the chili chocolate thins, put the semisweet chocolate into the top of a double boiler (or use a heatproof bowl set over a saucepan of gently simmering water) and heat until melted. Remove from the heat and stir in the chili powder.

3 Drop teaspoonfuls of the chocolate mixture onto two of the prepared baking sheets. Sprinkle a little edible glitter over the thins before the chocolate sets. Let set in a cool place, but not in the refrigerator, for 1–2 hours.

4 For the cardamom white chocolate thins, put the white chocolate into the top of a double boiler (or use a heatproof bowl set over a saucepan of gently simmering water) and heat until melted. Remove from the heat and stir in the cardamom and pistachios.

5 Drop teaspoonfuls of the white chocolate mixture onto the remaining two prepared baking sheets. Sprinkle the remaining chopped pistachios and a little edible glitter over the thins before the chocolate sets. Let set in a cool place, but not in the refrigerator, for 1–2 hours. Store in an airtight container in a cool, dry place for up to five days.

Mulled Wine

INGREDIENTS
serves 4

1 (750-milliliter) bottle red wine
1¾ ounces sherry
8 cloves
1 cinnamon stick
½ teaspoon ground allspice
2 tablespoons honey
1 orange, cut into wedges
1 lemon, cut into wedges

METHOD

1 Put the wine, sherry, cloves, cinnamon, allspice, and honey into a saucepan. Warm over low heat, stirring, until just starting to simmer, but do not let it boil.

2 Remove from the heat and pour through a strainer. Discard the cloves and cinnamon stick.

3 Return the pan to the heat with the orange and lemon wedges and warm gently. Pour into four warm heatproof glasses.

Cranberry Collins

INGREDIENTS
serves 1
1¾ ounces vodka
¾ ounce elderflower syrup
2½ ounces cranberry juice
club soda
lime slice and lime peel twist,
    to decorate

METHOD
1 Put cracked ice into
a cocktail shaker.

2 Pour in the vodka,
elderflower syrup, and
cranberry juice and shake
until well frosted.

3 Strain into a Collins glass
filled with cracked ice.

4 Fill up with club soda and
decorate with the lime slice
and peel.

Christmas Cranberry & Orange Pies

INGREDIENTS
makes 12 individual pies

butter, for greasing
1¾ cups frozen cranberries
1 tablespoon cornstarch
3 tablespoons freshly squeezed
    orange juice

2 star anise
¼ cup superfine sugar or
    granulated sugar, plus
    extra for sprinkling

1 ready-to-bake rolled dough
    pie crust, chilled
all-purpose flour, for dusting
milk, to glaze

METHOD

1 Preheat the oven to 350°F and lightly grease a 12-cup cupcake pan.

2 Put the still-frozen cranberries in a medium saucepan along with the cornstarch and orange juice. Add the star anise and cook, uncovered, over low heat, stirring from time to time, for 5 minutes, or until the cranberries have softened. Add the sugar and cook for an additional 5 minutes, then let stand to cool.

3 Roll out the pie dough thinly on a lightly floured surface. Using a fluted cookie cutter, stamp out 12 circles, each 2½ inches in diameter. Press these gently into the prepared pan, rerolling the scraps as needed. Squeeze any remaining scraps together and reserve.

4 Brush the top edges of the pastry shells with a little milk. Discard the star anise, then spoon in the filling.

5 Roll out the remaining pie dough thinly on a lightly floured surface. Using a fluted pastry wheel, cut thin strips of dough. Arrange these over each pie and brush with a little milk. Sprinkle with a little sugar. Bake in the preheated oven for 20 minutes, covering with aluminum foil after 10 minutes if the tops are browning too quickly. Let stand to cool in the pan for 10 minutes, then loosen with a blunt knife and transfer to a wire rack to cool. Serve warm or cold.

Baby Bellini

INGREDIENTS
serves 1
1¾ ounces peach juice
¾ ounce lemon juice
sparkling apple juice

METHOD
1 Pour the peach juice and
lemon juice into a chilled
champagne flute and
stir well.

2 Fill up with sparkling apple
juice and stir again.

Champagne Pick-Me-Up

INGREDIENTS
serves 1
1¾ ounces brandy
¾ ounce orange juice
¾ ounce lemon juice
dash grenadine
champagne, chilled

METHOD

1 Put cracked ice into a cocktail shaker.

2 Pour in the brandy, orange juice, lemon juice, and grenadine and shake vigorously until well frosted.

3 Strain into a wine glass.

4 Fill up with champagne.

Index